# OUR ST. LUCIA

By Gerry and Gale Bay

Published by Gerry and Gale Bay
at Amazon.com

©2018 Gerry and Gale Bay

All rights reserved. No part of this publication may be reproduced, stored in a retrieval system, or transmitted in any form or by any means, electronic, mechanical, photocopying recording, scanning, or otherwise except as permitted under Section 107 or 108 of the 1976 United States Copyright Act, without the prior written permission of the authors. Requests for permission should be addressed to:

Gerald Bay, 27 Newport St., Jamestown, RI 02835.

This book is licensed for your personal enjoyment only. Thank you for respecting the hard work of these authors.

# Table of Contents

INTRODUCTION ..................................................................... v
WHAT TO KNOW BEFORE YOU GO ...................................... 1
   Why St. Lucia? ..................................................................... 1
   Financial Information ......................................................... 2
   Transportation .................................................................... 2
   Communications ................................................................. 3
   Medical Info ........................................................................ 4
WHERE TO STAY .................................................................. 5
   Rodney Bay/Gros Islet ........................................................ 6
   Castries ................................................................................ 7
   Marigot Bay ......................................................................... 8
   The Pitons ........................................................................... 9
USUAL AND UNUSUAL THINGS TO DO ............................. 11
   Rodney Bay ........................................................................ 11
   Castries .............................................................................. 12
   Marigot Bay ....................................................................... 13
   Ti Kaye and Anse La Raye ................................................. 15
   Piton Area .......................................................................... 16
RECCOMENDED ITINERARY ............................................. 18
   ARRIVAL ............................................................................ 18
   DAY 1 (Resort Day) ........................................................... 20
   Day 2 (Ti Kaye Village) ...................................................... 21
   Day 3 (Drive to Pitons) ..................................................... 23
   Day 4 (The Market and Pink Plantation House) ............. 25
   Day 5 (Boat trip to the Pitons) ......................................... 27
   Day 6 (Rodney Bay and Lunch at Cap Maison) ............... 27
   Day 7 (Time to head back home to reality) .................... 28
CONCLUSION .................................................................... 30
ABOUT THE AUTHORS ...................................................... 31
OTHER BOOKS BY GALE AND GERRY BAY .................... 32
PHOTO GALLERY ............................................................... 33
   Rodney Bay ....................................................................... 33
   Castries .............................................................................. 35
   Marigot Bay ....................................................................... 36
   Pitons ................................................................................. 38
   Snorkeling ......................................................................... 40

# INTRODUCTION

Web searches and travel guides are full of good, general information about a place but it is often difficult to obtain specific, inside information on exactly where to go and what to do. Someone with local knowledge can be very helpful but such a person is hard to find.

We wrote this book to be as though you have a local friend in St. Lucia and you have called him/her to ask, "Hey, I'm thinking about coming to St. Lucia and want to maximize my experience. I know very little about St. Lucia so I need your local knowledge to help in getting me pointed in the right direction. I really need to know where to stay, where to go and what to do so that I have a great time and don't waste time doing something stupid!"

For many years, we've sailed the Caribbean islands aboard our Hylas 54 as well as onboard friends' yachts. Thus, we know the islands well. A book about our adventures, "Sailing the Caribbean Islands", can be found in iBook, Kindle and paperback formats through Apple and Amazon or as an eBook through Smashwords.

As the years have gone by, our love of the Caribbean and its people have only intensified. About 10 years ago, we decided to put down roots by buying an apartment on St. Lucia, our favorite island. The apartment is part of the Marigot Bay Resort and Marina and is used as hotel rooms when we are not there.

We come to St. Lucia every November and February and travel all over the island in our rental car. Thus, we know all of the fun things to do, good restaurants and adventures very well.

This book is intended for people who may have familiarized themselves somewhat with St. Lucia with web searches or the usual tourist guides and overviews and now want some guidance on really where to stay and what to do. We hope that our local knowledge will be helpful to you as you make decisions about your visit and enjoy this very special place.

Writing a book of this nature is presumptuous, of course, in that our tastes and interests may not align well with some of our readers. Some folks like to just sit on a beach and others like to get out and about to explore. Some want aggressive physical activities and others want to just sun themselves. We've tried to address a variety of interests but, at the same time, convey what we love to do based on our many years of experience here. Our "sample itinerary" near the end of the book is one that we have used with our many visitors both young and old and, without exception, they loved their experience.

We hope this book conveys to you just how special St. Lucia and its people are. If you follow our suggestions, we know you will have a great time and will leave with many fond memories of the St. Lucian people and the island's beauty!

# WHAT TO KNOW BEFORE YOU GO

## Why St. Lucia?

There are many reasons to select St. Lucia as your destination but first and foremost is that St. Lucians are the friendliest, nicest people in the Caribbean. They are brought up to love others and to be hospitable. They will make your stay most enjoyable. You can ask them anything and they will respond with a typical greeting of, "No problem."

The women are generally a little shy and the men are energetic and enthusiastic. Most importantly, they are happy. They may have little by Western developed country standards but then again, they don't need much. You will generally see them out and about enjoying the island's nature and life rather than locked up in their homes staring at their iPhones.

Their schoolchildren wear uniforms and the professional people in the Capital of Castries are very well dressed. You will seldom hear a child crying or demanding candy. They take good care of their island and you will not see a lot of trash floating around. You will, however, encounter the occasional stray goat and local island dog.

The weather is fantastic. You will have little fear of being hit by a hurricane as they typically follow a more northern track like hurricanes Irma and Maria. In season temperatures are typically in the low 80's by day and low 70's at night. While you may experience a passing shower you will seldom have a totally rainy day. Generally these showers pass quickly and then the sun comes out. The locals call the rain, "Liquid Sunshine".

Another reason is that the country is beautiful. It's very rugged and has a World Heritage Site called the Pitons. These are two mountains that jut up from the ocean on the island's southwest corner. And the water is crystal clear; you can see down many feet to the coral reefs. If you like to snorkel or dive then this is a superb place to visit.

And then there's Piton beer! You must have a Piton. It slides down ever so easily on a hot day and is very tasty indeed.

Finally, it's relatively easy to get to with nonstops from New York, Boston, Chicago and Atlanta and connections through Miami, Charlotte and other cities.

## Financial Information

The local currency is called Eastern Caribbean Dollars or EC. The EC is pegged at $1.00USD = 2.70 EC's. This works out to multiplying local prices by 0.37 to find out the USD price. It is easiest to just multiply by 0.4 to get the approximate price so that $25 EC is $10USD. You will find that US dollars will be taken everywhere and even preferred at some stores and restaurants.

Credit cards are taken everywhere but you'll need some EC's for local incidentals. There are ATM's nearby most resorts. While you can go to a bank to change dollars, that seems to be a bit of a hassle sometimes since there can be long lines. Check with your credit card company to make sure you don't have foreign currency translation fees and that they use the pegged EC rate. Also, make sure that you notify the credit card company ahead of time about your trip so that you don't have a fraud alert that shuts your card down.

Tipping is almost always included in your bill and typically runs 10%. Nobody expects more but be generous if you wish. If you're paying with cash, you may wish to leave the pocket change that you get when your change is returned.

## Transportation

There are three ways to get around the island: Driving, taxi and water taxi. While water taxi is fun, be prepared to get a little wet. Taxis offer the advantage of having a driver who knows his way around the twisty roads and is familiar with the local driving customs. They are, however, rather expensive.

We enjoy driving around St. Lucia. It gives us our freedom to come and go as we please and to visit multiple places while we have the car. However, be aware that the St Lucians drive on the left hand side of the road. If you're from the UK or its former or current territories, this will be no problem. If you're from the US, then it will only take you a little time until you get used to the new rules.

Driving in St. Lucia can be a bit of an experience. No one observes speed limits and they sometimes pass on curves or whenever they want. You will find yourself in a bit of a road race :-). It's not a problem but just take it slow and easy until you get in the flow and understand the "unwritten rules".

If you are planning to drive in St. Lucia, be sure to get an International Driver's License before you travel. They are inexpensive at AAA and if you don't have one, you will have to pay a hefty fee to the rental car agency for a local driver's license.

We typically rent from Drive-A-Matic. They are very responsive in terms of pick up and drop off times and locations. They are pretty persnickety, however, about an occasional scratch or bump on their cars.

## Communications

All of the resorts have wifi and it is adequate for email and basic uses. You can stream video but generally at standard definition rather than HD. It can be glitchy sometimes and, occasionally, wifi will go out for a while. While disruption of service is unusual, it can happen.

There is cellphone service island-wide but it can be spotty in the out areas because mountains and hills can block the signals. You should have no problem around the normal tourist areas and resorts. Check with your carrier about the need for an international plan. Some carriers, like T-Mobile, allow you to use your phone in St. Lucia seamlessly. Other carriers are more restrictive and expensive, however. If you'll be there for an extended period of time or plan to return, consider getting a basic local phone. If you don't have an international plan, then make sure that you have airplane mode on and disable data roaming so that you will not inadvertently run up a bill. Also, familiarize yourself with your phone's wifi calling capability.

## Medical Info

Medical care is basic and is provided by a variety of clinics spread around the island and one major hospital. The main hospital is called Tapion and is located on the outskirts of Castries towards Marigot Bay. There used to be another hospital called St. Judes in the South end of the island but it burned down and is now run more or less as a clinic out of a soccer stadium.

If you have an emergency, Tapion is capable of providing the initial care and then you will be airlifted to Martinique or the States. Anyone with a medical condition should consider staying in Marigot Bay, Castries or at some of the resorts just north of the airport on the Road to Rodney Bay so as to be close to the hospital. For minor issues, most resorts have a doctor on call.

# WHERE TO STAY

Your first consideration is to decide what kind of an experience you want. The northern part of the island is hilly but there is no comparison with the mountains of the rugged interior from the central coast south. So, if natural beauty is high on your list then Marigot Bay and the Pitons area should be considered. However, if you want to be near the largest beach on the island, then the Rodney Bay area may be your choice although it's a very busy, commercial area and there are several beautiful, less crowded beaches further south.

Most of the resorts on the island are on the Western coast. The east faces the prevailing trade winds so the water tends to be rough making water sports difficult. The West side has gentler winds because it is somewhat shielded by the mountains and the waters are calmer making for a very pleasant experience. However, when there are strong easterly winds that kick up a big swell, these swells can bend around the top and bottom of the island and come into the beaches. This is particularly true at the northern end of the island and sometimes the Rodney Bay area has rougher surf than the middle of the island around Marigot Bay.

There are many types of accommodations on the island including Villas, All-Inclusive, Resorts and condos. While All-Inclusives are popular, they give you a somewhat limited view of St. Lucia. You really need to get out and about to experience the island's pleasures.

Many of the resorts have been built with investor-owned apartments that are part of the rental pool when the owner is not there. You will find great bargains at top-notch resorts by checking in with Flip Key or Trip Advisor since some apartment owners advertise their rooms for rent to make a little money on the side. If you choose to do that, make sure that this is allowed under the terms of the owner's rental pool agreement.

Be a little cautious about the reviews and ratings on sites like Trip Advisor. There are several highly rated resorts that we would rate differently than what is shown. Also, be aware that most of the pools at the resorts are on the small side.

There are four primary areas to stay in St. Lucia. From north to south they are: Rodney Bay/Gros Islet, Castries, Marigot Bay and the Pitons. While there are other areas, they are off the beaten path. Our favorite area is Marigot Bay (Full disclosure: We have an apartment there as part of the Marigot Bay Resort and Marina) but here are what we believe are the pluses and minuses of each area.

## Rodney Bay/Gros Islet

This is the area where most visitors to the island tend to go because it is well developed with numerous resorts and restaurants. The big attraction is a beautiful two-mile long beach and a large marina where it is fun to "boat watch". However, the popularity of this area means that it is crowded and busy. The road connecting the resorts, activities and restaurants is usually packed with stop and go traffic. The resorts are nice and many have their own beaches. But be aware that it could take 30-45 minutes at times to get to Castries and the market. And a trip to the Pitons is probably close to two hours away. However, if beaching, hustle and bustle, crowds and nightlife are your thing then this is the "go to" place.

The beach is spectacular but sometimes overly crowded with cruise ship passengers smoking cigars, etc. You can rent beach chairs and umbrellas and can buy trinkets from the locals that ply the beach. They can, however, be rather aggressive. The water here is warm and swimmable but is not as clear as in other parts of the island and there's not much snorkeling here.

There is a large marina here and it's fun to "boat watch". There are not many marine facilities in the Caribbean so the Rodney Bay Marina is a big draw for pleasure boats from all over the world. There are restaurants all around the Marina where you can sit and watch the comings and goings. You can also book sunset sails and boating adventures here including a large "pirate ship".

The Rodney Bay Mall, near the Marina, features many nice shops such as the Sea Island Cotton Shop, our favorite. The Treasure Bay Casino is also a fun place if gambling is on your agenda.

There are many resorts around the Marina, most of which are decent. But our favorite resort would be Cap Maison that is just north of Rodney Bay and is thus a little more quiet and secluded. It is located on a cliff with beautiful views of Pigeon Island and Martinique and it has a little secluded beach at the base with a bar and restaurant. Another special resort is East Winds (Very intimate and highly rated) just South of Rodney Bay.

Three others to consider are Calabash Cove just South of Rodney Bay, The Landings just North of the Marina and Body Holiday near Cap Maison. However, these three are all more or less typical resorts that you might find most anywhere rather than the special, intimate Caribbean-type of experience. You will find service at these resorts to be a little less personal than at the Boutique resorts.

If golf is your thing, then look into the villas at Cap Estates, which are very nice.

## Castries

Castries is a busy commercial center and is where the cruise ships dock. There's a fun market there with veggies and souvenir stands. Most of the hotels are just North of the local airport, Viggie (SLU), on the busy road to Rodney Bay. However, the most prominent one, which is just to the South of Castries, is Sandals Le Toc. It's an all-inclusive that is popular with honeymooners and is the one we like the best of the three Sandals resorts on the island. The people who stay here often don't get to experience the "real" St. Lucia" because they tend to stay in the all-inclusive resort rather than getting out and about. However, Le Toc has a number of good restaurants and shops.

There is a new accommodation just opening up in the 2017-18 season called the Pink Plantation House. It's high up on the mountain overlooking Castries and our favorite St. Lucian restaurant operates out of there. They have a few guest bedrooms and Michelle, the owner, is delightful and would do anything to accommodate you.

There are two resorts that are highly rated on Trip Advisor that we feel compelled to provide you with a little more info:

The Rendezvous is located right at the end of the airport runway and behind an auto dealership and shop.  At the southern end of their beach is a cemetery right on the ocean.

The Villa Beach Cottages are located right on the busy, noisy highway to Rodney Bay and there is little parking.

## Marigot Bay

About a third of the way down the western shore is a Bay that the author, James Michener, called, "The prettiest Bay in the Caribbean".  It is where the movie, "Dr. Doolittle", was filmed and is our favorite part of the island.  As you approach the Bay, you will have views of the large mountains in the island's interior.  In addition to its spectacular natural beauty, the Bay has the advantage of being centrally located so trips to other areas of the island are very easy.

There is a quaint little beach that is reachable directly or by a ferry that goes all of about a hundred yards depending on which side of the Bay your resort is on.  On the beach you'll find beach chairs and an activities booth where you can rent 21-foot keelboats, catamarans, paddleboards, kayaks, etc.  If the local behind the booth is not too busy, he'll even hop into a boat and "race" you.  They also conduct sailing and diving lessons.

The Bay is full of boats on moorings and you can go on day or sunset cruises.  Many mega-yachts tie up at the dock and it's fun to stroll along the docks watching the rich and famous enjoy their rewards.  There is also a nice hiking trail up the ridge across the Bay

There are several resorts in the Bay with the major one being the Marigot Bay Resort and Marina where we have our apartment.  In 2018, as this is written, they received the Travel + Leisure Magazine's award for being one of the 25 best resorts in the Caribbean, Bahamas and Bermuda.  They have one of the largest pools in St. Lucia and their spa is known for its superb service and friendly staff.

There are many nice restaurants in the Bay giving it a "neighborhood" feel.  While there is entertainment at the various resorts and restaurants during high season, it does tend to be quieter than Rodney Bay, which is either an advantage or disadvantage depending on your interests.

Marigot Bay can be slightly wetter than other parts of the island.  However, this has to be put in the context of the weather patterns that typically consist of an occasional passing shower lasting 5 minutes or so and then a sunny spell for a lot longer.  An extra brief shower or two has never felt like a big deal to us because the sun is out most of the time.  Also, a late day shower will produce a spectacular, horizon-to-horizon rainbow that is often a double one.

Just south of Marigot Bay is a resort called Ti Kaye.  It has a gorgeous beach, like on a picture post card, and good snorkeling.  However, it's rather isolated and hard to get in and out of on a very rugged, steep road.  We tend to think of it as a great day-trip for lunch and a snorkel but if isolation and natural beauty are high on your list, than this is a good choice.  The snorkeling is one of our three favorite spots on the island.

## The Pitons

For scenic beauty, the Pitons cannot be beat.  Oprah Winfrey has called them one of the "must stay" places on her bucket list.  The Pitons are two mountains that have pushed up from the seabed and they dominate the views wherever you go in the area.  Their beauty is simply breathtaking!

The only drive-in volcano in the Caribbean is in this area...indeed, most of the area is located within the old Caldera of the volcano.  When you drive into the volcano, there is a ticket booth and some souvenir stands where the locals will try to sell you a necklace.  Then, you drive in a few hundred yards and take a walking tour right up to the area where there is volcanic activity.

The main town, Soufrierre, is a bit rough and tough with some drug issues but can be fun during the day if you use normal precautions.  Nearby are waterfalls and a botanical garden, which are fun to visit.

There are some great resorts here with views of the Pitons but they tend to be expensive and the area is pretty isolated.  For example, if you want to visit the market in Castries, it is about an hour and a half or more away on a very twisty mountain road.  Among our favorite resorts are:
- The Ladera Resort that overlooks both Pitons. It is located high up in the "saddle" between the

two Pitons. You will feel like these mountains are right in your lap. The rooms are open walled and some have pools and brooks inside. The Dasheen restaurant at the resort is spectacular.
- Sugar Beach is right at the base of the Pitons and has an idyllic beach and little cottages tucked into the hillside. Snorkeling the base of the Petite Piton is one of our top three sites. The resort has a fairly large presence from its security detail and they seem to be hovering around at all times. While this is comforting, it seems like a little overkill to us.
- Jade Mountain where "The Bachelor" was taped is another favorite. It has a more long distance view of the Pitons and open sided walls.
- The Anse Chastanet Resort is on the water around the corner from the Pitons and does not have a direct view. However, it is a very pretty setting with a nice beach and cottages tucked away into the jungle. The snorkeling here is among our top three spots.

We frequently drive down from Marigot Bay to have lunch and to snorkel at these resorts. The trip takes about an hour or slightly more. The views, after all, are mainly in the day when it is light.

# USUAL AND UNUSUAL THINGS TO DO

Each of the four areas of St. Lucia has some really fun things to do and some cool restaurants. Here's our list of favorite things to do in the various areas of the island.

## Rodney Bay

- Lunch at Spinnakers. This is a beach shack kind of place and it's just funky. There are sailboat pictures all over the restaurant and you can enjoy the bathing beauties on the beach. Enter the Rodney Bay Mall road and proceed until it takes a right hand curve. At the police station take a left and proceed to the waterfront.
- Just north of Spinnakers on the beach is a stand where a lady sells homemade Roti's that are delicious. A Roti is curried chicken in a wrap and is an island favorite.
- In the Marina, check out Elena's where they have the best ice cream/gelato/sorbet on the island. They also have a shop in the Rodney Bay Mall area.
- On the north side of the Marina is a road that takes you back to where the fisherman come in with their catch at the harbor entrance. It's definitely a "local color" place to watch them unload and dress fish. The entrance to the road is by the ECHF sign.
- Lunch at The Cliff at Cap in the Cap Maison resort north of Rodney Bay is very special. You can watch sailboats coming over or going to Martinique and even see the island on a clear day. They also have a lower level restaurant on a sweet little beach that belongs to the resort. Idyllic!
- Another good restaurant is Jacques where you will dine overlooking the entrance to the marina.

- In the Rodney Bay Mall area there are some nice shops for the ladies such as the Sea Island Cotton shop.

## Castries

- The big attraction here is the Market. It is teeming with T-shirt and souvenir shops. It is relatively safe...we have never had any problems...but as with any third world country you need to be aware of the potential for pick pockets. As you enter the main market on the west side go back in several rows and on your left you will meet Mr. G...a jovial fellow who has some nice carved wood pieces. Also, there are some nice paintings by local artists in this building. As you continue through you will reach the vegetable area and it's fun to see all the strange local veggies. Finally, at the northern end, you will find the fish market. It's a hoot. Make sure you bargain for souvenirs. You should be able to get around a quarter to a third off the opening asking price.
- Going into the town itself, you will find a large local church, public square, etc. that are worthwhile to see.
- Two of our favorite restaurants are in the Castries area: The Pink Plantation House and the Coal Pot. They are both owned and operated by Michelle Elliott and feature truly authentic Caribbean cuisine. Michelle is also a local artist and you will see her beautiful, colorful pottery featured at the restaurant and around the island at selected shops.
- The Coal Pot is on the water and is very romantic at night. If they have Red Snapper on the menu, order it...you won't be disappointed!
- We can't recommend the Pink Plantation House highly enough. It is our favorite restaurant. It's up high on the mountain overlooking Castries and is a little hard to find...better take a cab. In addition to the spectacular views all the way out to Martinique, the food is authentic, delicious and reasonably priced. Our favorite is the curried chicken in a

coconut shell. It's not like what you might find in an American restaurant. It's not "hot spicy" but has many pleasant flavors. It is served with a vegetable tray of local veggies such as christophene. You'll love the atmosphere of gentle winds rustling through the palm trees and listening to the "squeaks" of the Banana Quit birds.
- While you are at the Pink Plantation House, go to the Caribelle Batik store that is nearby. In addition to the nice clothes for sale, be sure to stop by on the outside lower level. There you will find a little demonstration by locals as to how chocolate and coconut oil is made. They are very friendly and enthusiastic and are proud to tell the tale. Be sure to buy some chocolate. It tastes different than you may be used to but that's because it's natural cocoa without all the preservatives and things that we are used to. Delicious! The views here are also stunning.
- Leaving the Pink Plantation House and the Batik store, come down the mountain towards Marigot Bay and you'll find "Eudovics Art Gallery". The finest woodcarvings on the island are here and you can purchase anything from a local mask wall hanging to gorgeous contemporary figures. Mr. Eudovic is a pleasant old character and his daughter, Dawn, is extraordinarily nice. They also have an interesting wood carving demo and talk in their workshop. They also have a bar and the sign out front used to say "Eudovic's Art Gallery and Bar", which always made us chuckle!

# Marigot Bay

- As you come into Marigot Bay from the main road, you will go up a hill and then down towards the water and the resorts. Be sure to stop at the top of the hill to get a great view of the beautiful Bay and a preview of what is in store for you. You may be hounded by locals trying to sell you birds and baskets made from palm fronds but either fend them off or support the local economy by tipping

them $5EC. The view is well worth any minor aggravation.
- Getting around the Bay is generally by a little ferry that stops at the beach and various resorts and restaurants. Early in your trip, it's fun to hop on and just take a tour around the Bay. Generally, the ride is free but you may wish to tip the driver $5EC or so. All stops are close to each other...only a few yards away.
- There are numerous restaurants in the Bay. Unfortunately, one of the best ones on St. Lucia, The Rainforest Hideaway, has closed recently due to the owner's retirement. The main resort in the Bay is The Marigot Bay Resort and Marina. Their "The Grill" dining room features fine dining with a nice view of the Marina. Other restaurants in the resort are the Rum Cave that features rum tasting and the Hurricane Hole that features sandwiches down by the Ferry dock.
- The Oasis resort, reachable by ferry, has a restaurant called Doolittle's and it is a good place to enjoy a drink and watch the sun set although service can be slow and food quality has its ups and downs. They have pool tables for fun if you get tired of the views.
- Another good spot is the Chateau Mygo by Capella that features thin crust pizzas in addition to local fare like fish and Roti's.
- Pirate Cove, which used to be called JJ's and then JD's, has decent food but can be a little buggy.
- There's also a highly rated Indian restaurant, Masala, located on the second floor above the Hurricane Hole by the Ferry dock. The food is spicy but quite tasty.
- Finally, there is a new bar and restaurant that just opened in the previous Rainforest location. Reachable by ferry, Hassey's is populated by friendly locals and tourists as well.
- Any of the resorts can provide you with the usual sunset cruises, zip line tours, etc. but for a really fun local experience, look up a local called Denver or Sava. You can find him on the beach, by the

ferry dock or via his website, http://www.shashamane.co. He is a wonderful island character and a genuinely nice guy. He makes the best rum punch on the island. Sava runs a water taxi service but what's really fun is his tour to the Pitons. He will take you along the coastline and explain all the local sites including the bat cave. He will drop you at the Sugar Beach resort at the base of the Pitons for lunch and wait while you snorkel the Pitons. Just a really fun day!
- The Marina is part of the Marigot Bay Resort and Marina and is often filled with Mega-yachts. You can watch notables like Jeff Bezos, CEO of Amazon, dine on the stern of their yachts as you walk the docks or enjoy a meal in your room at the resort. Catch the name of the yacht and then Google it and you'll get a run down on its particulars.
- There's a terrific hike up the mountain behind the Oasis resort. Ask the locals how to find the entrance and path. Great views!
- You can rent beach toys, kayaks and Sunfishes from a vendor on the beach.

## Ti Kaye and Anse La Raye

- Pretty much all by itself is the beautiful, laid back Ti Kaye resort...one of our favorites to visit for lunch but pretty isolated from other island activities. The entrance road winds up and down hills on very rough and rutty roads. However, once you are there, they have a restaurant on top of a bluff with great ocean views. But our favorite is the beach "shack" down on the water. Here you will find one of the prettiest coves on the island and one of the best sites to snorkel.
- Nearby Ti Kaye is the fishing village of Anse La Raye. It is full of local flavor and looks like a page out of the musical, Porgy and Bess. Just driving through is a hoot. On Fridays, the locals put on a fish fry that is a fun outing!
-

# Piton Area

- St. Lucia has the only drive-in volcano in the Caribbean and it's a fun stop. The locals will tell you its history and you can watch the "plop-plops" and smell the sulfur. Be sure to get them to tell you the story of Gabriel, a tour guide who fell through the crust! Also, there are mud baths that are fun and refreshing. You will find some fairly aggressive locals here selling beaded necklaces, etc. But just enjoy the local flavor and buy a Christmas present. These people are from the surrounding area and it's nice to patronize them.
- Your trip to St. Lucia will not be complete without seeing the spectacular Pitons. The best place to see them is at the Dasheen Restaurant at the Ladera Resort that is located on a ridge between the two mountains. The views are simply breathtaking and the food is delicious. Be sure to listen to the squeaky song of the Banana Quit bird here. Very unique.
- After lunch at Dasheen, go up the hill and across the road to the Boucan Restaurant in the Hotel Chocolate Resort. Located in a chocolate plantation, the restaurant features a chocolate sampler that will blow the mind of any chocolate aficionado! It's a great place to finish off the meal that you just ate at Dasheen.
- Sugar Beach at the base of the Pitons is another fantastic view spot. The beach is gorgeous, the snorkeling is great and views are incomparable. It looks like the travel brochures! As you drive in, you'll be stopped at a guard gate and he will instruct you to the parking lot that is still quite a ways up the hill from the beach. Golf cart service to the beach is spotty so you may be in for a bit of a hike. We have found the land entrance to this resort to be a little stand-offish in the past but, hopefully, those problems have been resolved. We enjoy coming to the beach and restaurant via water taxi rather than driving and they are very

accommodating when you arrive this way. (See Marigot Bay).
- Other fun adventures include the Diamond Botanical Gardens, the Toraille Waterfall and walking around the local fishing village called Soufriere.

# RECCOMENDED ITINERARY

We often have visitors and have developed an itinerary that gives them the true St. Lucia experience. It is a balance between enjoying the pool, beach and resort and getting out and about to see the island and to experience the wonderful St. Lucian culture.

The itinerary we'll discuss below involves driving to see various sights but you can also do the itinerary by taxi. The itinerary assumes that you are staying at a resort in Marigot Bay such as the Marigot Bay Resort and Marina. Certainly, it can be adjusted to wherever you are located on the island but seeing all of the sites is easiest if you stay somewhere in Marigot Bay because it is centrally located.

## ARRIVAL

When you make your plane reservations, make sure you get window seats on the left side of the aircraft looking forward. That way you will get a magnificent view of the Pitons as you are approaching the island for a landing. Also, when you book your flight, try to get one with an arrival time before 3 PM. At that hour, there are usually a number of flights that land all at about the same time including a 747 from London. This results in some fairly long lines at the Customs and Immigration area.

After retrieving your bags and clearing the customs area, you will be hounded by "Red Caps" that will offer to handle your bags for you. Unless you have lots of stuff, you will not need them to help you cover the 15 yards to the outer world. They basically pick up your bags, go 50 feet through some doors and then drop them on the other side.

As you exit through the doors, you'll find a number of stands about 20 feet in front of you with signs indicating what resort they represent. The person at the stand will take care of getting you to your resort taxi. Some stands, such as the Marigot Bay Resort and Marina, will have a very nice lady who will offer you a cold washcloth and take your order for a drink upon your arrival at the resort. Some resorts do not have stands but you should find a person with a card with your name on it and they will greet you and take care of you.

If you are renting a car, proceed further on and you'll see various rent-a-car booths. They will take you to your car and do all the paper work. We recommend getting the insurance because you don't need any hassles in a third world country. Some car companies have a quirk in that sometimes they want a letter from your doctor that you are competent to drive. Also, make sure that you do a complete inspection with the agent and, perhaps, even take some pictures especially underneath the front fender. In the US, the rental companies are not fussy about a scratch here and there but they are in St. Lucia.

The drive to the hotel will take you about 1 hour or a little more if you're going to Marigot Bay or the Pitons and slightly more if you're going to Rodney Bay. You can't get lost if you're going to Marigot Bay because there are only two turns and you can't miss them. As you begin driving, you will find that you are in a Sports Car Rally or Road Race rather than what you might think of as a pleasant drive on a country road. They think nothing of passing on curves at high speed so be alert.

After 15 minutes or so, you'll see a sign on the left for the Fox Grove Inn. Keep going straight ahead. You will be heading down a hill towards the water. Then you will begin climbing again. After 25-30 minutes from the airport, you will be in a sweeping left hand curve with some restaurant/bar-type shacks on the right. It is on the side of a cliff overlooking a spectacular view of the ocean. You must stop here and have a Piton...the local beer that we think is the best in the world. Whether or not you are a beer drinker, you will find that an occasional Piton during the week will keep you in that mellow Caribbean spirit as will the ubiquitous rum drinks

Continue on while dodging the occasional goat, chicken and stray dog...it is the Caribbean after all. Enjoy going through the pass in the rain forest where you will see gigantic fern leaves. Eventually, you will reach a T in the road. Turn left. You'll find a grocery store on your left about a quarter mile away. Stop and get supplies if you want and, of course, some Piton beer and some wine. The wine selection on the island is not great but we generally get a brand called

"Sunrise" or "120". Both the Chardonnay and the Merlot are at least drinkable with minimal damage to your throat. However, save your receipt as we have occasionally had a bad bottle. The selection of foods at this store is not up to US standards but you'll find pretty much everything you will need.

Outside the supermarket is a vegetable stand and you might want to check on their offerings. Avocados are generally good and you may find some mangoes in season.

Continue on and go up and over the "mini-mountain" ahead. The only tricky part of the trip is near the top where there seems to be a Y in the road. Do not go straight but take the sweeping right turn and head down the hill. At the bottom of the hill is the entrance road to Marigot Bay. You will see a lot of signs there marking it. If you go past a soccer field with speed bumps, you've gone too far.

Take the right hand turn into Marigot Bay. The road is a little rough. At the top of the hill, there will be a bar on the left but there's a little parking area on the right. Stop there and take a look at the view of the Bay. It should be near sunset and will be very pretty.

Continue on down to the Marigot Bay Resort and Marina entrance on the right or to the parking lots on the left if you are going to take the ferry to another resort across the Bay. You will find the welcome folks at any of the resorts around the Bay very pleasant and accommodating. At the Marigot Bay Resort and Marina, you will receive a cold washcloth and a rum drink to enjoy and to get you in the proper spirit!

After you settle in to your room, you will be pretty tired from your trip. We'd recommend that you have dinner at the resort or you may wish to avail yourselves of room service. If you're at the Marigot Bay Resort and Marina, go down past the pool to the central area and then go downstairs to the Rum Cave area. You'll find a nice little cafe by the waterside.

## DAY 1 (Resort Day)

Today will be a Resort Day because you will be tired from your trip. You'll probably sleep in. You'll find as the week goes on you will have a later and later start! Caribbean sleeping sickness! Have a cup of coffee on the deck and relax.

Please note that you are only 13 degrees north of the equator and you can get a sunburn in a matter of a few minutes so it's a good idea to get out the sunblock if you're heading to the pool. This is a good morning to walk the docks along the Marina and to have breakfast at the Hurricane Hole near the Ferry dock.

Make sure you listen for the various bird songs, which are much different from your home area. There's a pretty little yellow-breasted bird called the Banana Quit, which is one of our favorites because of its squeaky little voice.

After breakfast, take the Ferry over to the beach. Go to the water sports desk and inquire about renting snorkel gear. Also, ask around to see if Sava (aka Denver) is around. He's a truly nice Caribbean character and a good friend. He does boat trips to the Pitons, etc. and we'll talk about him later on in this write-up. He hangs out over there sometimes. If you find him, discuss plans for a boat trip to the Pitons.

Upon returning to your room, make reservations for the various activities of the week ahead. It would be good to check in with your resort's activities desk to see what activities might be available that are not covered in this book. There is much to do such as a Zip Line through the jungle, water park, ATV adventures, go-kart track, etc. However, these are shoestring operations and tend to go in and out of business frequently so they are not specifically covered in this book.

The rest of the day, explore and relax by the pool. Rest up for the big adventures ahead. A little "Toes Up" in the PM is very much in keeping with the Caribbean pace.

Tonight may be a good night to go to Chateau Mygo near the hotel. If you don't go tonight, see what night they have music.

## Day 2 (Ti Kaye Village)

By now you will have slowed down enough that you will have trouble getting going anytime before noon so we'll make this an easy day. Pack your snorkel gear in the car and pick up some towels at the front reception desk. Wear your bathing suits and a top. Leave the resort around 11:30-12 and take the road back to the highway. Turn right. Go through the banana plantations and up and down the hills.

You'll go through a town called Anse La Raye....it's right out of Porgy and Bess. Go through very slowly so you don't miss any of the sights!

After more up and down hills, you will eventually come to Ti Kaye....there's a big sign there so you can't miss it. You'll need to take a right hand turn into the entrance road but it's difficult to make because there can be unseen traffic coming in from the left. Meeting a cement truck careening down the hill can ruin your day. We actually wait until there is no traffic behind us and then my wife, Gale, hops out where she can see up the hill and then she waves me across.

Now for a real adventure! The road is nearly impassable with ruts and potholes but don't get discouraged because the secluded little beach at the end is well worth it! Keep on keeping on. You will eventually reach a guard shack and you'll wonder if you're out of place coming in there. But don't worry; the guard is usually quite jovial. Tell the guard that you're there to have lunch on the beach and that you know you have to sign in at the front desk.

After you clear the gate, go straight ahead to the resort. Go to the front desk where you pay $10 each as a prepaid lunch chit. Then you drive back towards the guard shack but go to the left of it. You will now go down a hill that may give you pause because it's so steep. But, not to fear, it's all doable and it is the Caribbean after all. At the bottom is a beach shack restaurant overlooking a fantastic beach. It's a picture postcard of what you think the Caribbean looks like and vegging out here will make the trip worth it. It's one of our favorite places and definitely worth the effort.

The food is simple but good. Our favorites would be the fish, rice and salad or the Roti. (The Roti is an island favorite and is sort of curried chicken stew in a wrap). Be sure to order a basket of "Local Chips or Vegetable Chips". After lunch, with the obligatory Piton, you will have mellowed out so much that you may not want to move but...it's time to head to the car to get the snorkel gear. As you exit the beach shack, check out the nearby flagpole and identify the color of the flag. If it's green or yellow, you're fine but if it's red then there might be some rough surf. It's still generally ok to snorkel when the flag is red if you are fit but you may find the water to be a little cloudy. It would be best to leave your money and ID's in your locked car rather than on the beach.

As you have lunched, you may have noted that a catamaran or two have arrived and dumped their load of people into the water. They generally clear out by 2 or 3 PM and then you will have the snorkel area pretty much to yourselves. You'll also find that the snorkeling is particularly beautiful later in the afternoon when the sun gets lower in the sky and the light filters through the water.

Head down the beach to the far end and in you go. Along the way you may find some locals that will try to sell you some things. Enjoy the interaction or just tell them you aren't interested.

The snorkeling here is excellent and we occasionally see squid, eels, octopus, etc. in addition to all the brightly colored reef fish. Make sure you snorkel all the way out to the point because there are some beautiful fans out there waving in the current. It's very protected and, because of the salt water, you will float with no effort. After drying off and putting on a dry top, it's time to drive back up the hill...close your eyes...and back to the resort.

Dinner tonight is local...see the restaurant discussion in "Usual and Unusual Things To Do"

## Day 3 (Drive to Pitons)

Make a 12:30 reservation at the Dasheen restaurant at the Ladera resort (758-459-7323) and leave Marigot Bay about 11 AM. Head out like you're going to Ti Kaye. Stop along the way when you see a snake charmer and get your picture taken for $5 or $10 EC. (EC =USD X 0.4) Your kids or grandkids will love it and admire you greatly!

The drive to the Pitons is very pretty. You will pass through some quaint fishing villages and see the very rugged mountains of the interior. The road is generally good, at least by Caribbean standards. However, be alert for potholes that can sometimes be quite large.

As you travel along, enjoy seeing the various microclimates on the island. You can be looking at cactus one minute and big, rain forest ferns the next. It may be tempting to stop along the way for photo ops, particularly of the little fishing villages. However, you will get better pictures on the way home as the sun will be behind you and the colored houses in the towns will glow.

As you come into the Piton area you will go through a narrow road on the side of the mountain and some rain forest areas. You will eventually come to a downhill road coming into the town of Soufriere and there will be magnificent views of the Pitons. There are two great turnoffs for picture taking if you can get through the tour busses and the swarm of souvenir hawkers. There is not much parking space at the first turnoff but the view is great. The second turnoff has more parking and a pavilion from which to view the Pitons.

Continue on to the town of Soufriere, which means "sulfur in the air"...a reference to the nearby volcano. After you go across the bridge, the oncoming road is one-way towards you so you will take a left and then the next right. Just keep following this road past the church and up the hill.

After a few miles, you will see the entrance to the volcano on your left. Continue in to the gate and buy tickets and then drive on up. Take the guided tour, which is generally quite interesting and informative. You'll learn that the whole "miles across" area including Soufriere is part of the Caldera. Make sure they tell you the story of Gabriel, the tour guide who fell into the boiling water.

After leaving the volcano, turn left. The Ladera resort is just a little way up in the saddle between the Pitons and is a great spot for lunch. As you walk from the parking area to the restaurant, notice the 9/11 memorial that they have erected and listen for the squeaking Banana Quit birds that are quite prevalent here. The views from the Dasheen restaurant are simply breathtaking. You'll look out right at the Pitons and feel like you can almost touch them. You'll be up high and be able to look down at the resort at Sugar Beach. Cruising boats will be on the moorings offshore of the beach but you are so high that they look very tiny.

After lunch, if it's not too late, go to the main road and turn right for a few hundred feet to the Boucan Restaurant at the Hotel Chocolate. It's in a chocolate plantation and the restaurant can show you the cocoa fruit. The views are also good and you've got to have one of their chocolate sampler specialties.

The trip home is pleasant and you will have many photo ops along the way. In particular, as you approach the village of Canaries, there is an area to pull off that gives you a great view of the multicolored houses. They will be all lit up in the late day sun.

## Day 4 (The Market and Pink Plantation House)

After our big day yesterday, we'll have an easy day today. In the morning, we'll go into Castries and explore the market. It's great fun to walk around and experience the local sights and smells. Then it's lunch at the Pink Plantation House (758-452-5422)--our favorite St. Lucian restaurant.

You'll want to leave around 10:30 to 11 to make a 12:30 to 1 lunch reservation. As you leave Marigot Bay and get to the main road, go left. When you get to the supermarket that you saw on the way in, go another 100 yards and take a left. Follow the road into town.

At the second roundabout, take the second exit and proceed along the waterfront. You'll come to a light and bear left along with most of the traffic. Continue to follow the road into town until you get to a big intersection on the edge of the market. Take a left and go to the next roundabout. Go about 3/4 of the way around and you will see a supermarket on the left. At the far end of the supermarket there is a driveway. Take a left into the driveway and you'll see the entrance to the parking garage. The market is across the street from the supermarket.

When done wandering around, go back to the parking garage and take a right after leaving. Then take a left at the roundabout and then a right at the far end of the market. Go down a few hundred yards to a stoplight and take a left. You will know you are correct if you are on a 4-lane road with a large center divider. Take this road over the bridge and then up the side of the mountain.

When you pass the Governor's Mansion you will be close to the turnoff to the Pink Plantation House. You will see a small sign on the left and it will be a small angle left turn. There will be several intersections but at each one you will see a Pink Plantation House sign. The road becomes narrow and rough but not at all as bad as Ti Kaye.

Eventually, you will see the left turn into the Pink Plantation House. Ask for Michelle, the Owner, and give her our regards. If she's not there today, then Tito or Kim will take care of you.  Enjoy the fantastic view over a couple of Pitons.  All food is good but we particularly like the curried chicken in a coconut shell.  We're usually not big curry fans but this curry is really different and authentic Caribbean food and we love it.  You will also get a big dish of interesting Caribbean veggies.  Get Tito to show you the Christophene...it's terrific.  There's plenty of food so you can take half your lunch home and have it for dinner.

Make sure you look at Michelle's pottery work, which is for sale in the next room.  It's really colorful and beautiful and gives you the great St. Lucian flavor.

After those Pitons and a big lunch, it's time to head back to Marigot Bay for some "Toes Up".  But first, there are a couple of really interesting stops to make on the way home.  There's a Batik shop nearby that has some nice things and also has a very interesting demonstration of chocolate making.  As you leave the Pink Plantation House, take a right to the first intersection and then take another right.  Go until the road dead ends and then take a left.  The Batik shop is a few hundred yards down on your left.

Walk down the steps into the shop.  There's usually a steel drum man playing here and it's a nice touch.  The ladies will want to shop a bit here.  After that is complete, go down another level onto the back porch.  There you will have another fantastic view of the island and the Caribbean Sea.  On a nice day, you can see all the way to Martinique.

At the far end of the porch are two rooms manned by locals.  They will give you an interesting demo of chocolate making in one room and coconut oil in the other.

On the way back you'll want to make a stop at Eudovic's Art Gallery featuring native wood working sculptures with special native woods.

Go back to the main road the way you came in and take a left to continue on over the mountain.  As you go down the other side...about half way down...you'll see his sign on the right.  Pull in and they will give you a brief presentation about their woodworking.  Then visit their showroom across the road where you will find everything from souvenirs to gorgeous wood sculptures.  Ask for Eudovic's daughter, Dawn.  She's a delight.  Mr. Eudovic is elderly but if he's there, he's fun to talk with.  The wood they use is a rare local wood and get them to tell you about it.

After leaving, take a right at the main road and continue down the mountain. You will reach a familiar intersection but just keep going straight up, over and down the "mini-mountain" to Marigot Bay.

## Day 5 (Boat trip to the Pitons)

Even though you have already driven to the Pitons, this will be a totally different experience. Meet Sava on the dock at 11 AM and he'll take care of the rest. Bring cash, USD, for him and a credit card for lunch. No need to dress up. Beachwear is fine. He will take you along the shoreline and tell you many interesting tales. Make sure he shows you the bat cave.

As you come into the Pitons, Sava will drop you at the beach and then wait for you. The beach is one of the prettiest in St. Lucia and is right at the base of the Pitons...a truly spectacular view.

Lunch will be on the beach at the restaurant or at the tables in the sand near the bar. After lunch, snorkel the base of the Pitons. Again, this is a fantastic area teeming with colorful fish and coral.

When you're done snorkeling, get a Piton and relax on the beach chairs to the left of the dock. These chairs are free unlike the resort chairs on the main beach. Then, when you're ready, wave at Sava who will be on a mooring or anchored just off the end of the dock. On the way back home, try some of Sava's home made rum punch...it's delicious! Also, make sure you take pictures with the Pitons in the background. You'll be home around 4 PM.

This would be a good night to dine at the Coal Pot (758-452-5566) near the airport in Castries. It's one of our top two restaurants and is on the water and very romantic. It's also run by Michelle so if you missed her at Pink Plantation, you might see her here. The Coal Pot is a "must go" destination sometime during your stay. We love the Coquille St. Jaques and the Red Snapper and again the food is authentic Caribbean.

## Day 6 (Rodney Bay and Lunch at Cap Maison)

This is sort of an optional day. If you're exhausted, then hang out at the resort and try the sushi at the pool.

If you're young and athletic, then try the Zip Line or ATV tours or take a hike up the trail behind the Oasis Marigot.

Otherwise, it's worth it to complete your island experience to head up to Rodney Bay where you will see the Marina and the Beach. It will take about 45 minutes to get up there where we'll make an interim stop and then another 10 minutes or so to Cap Maison for lunch.

Proceed into Castries as before but continue through the roundabout rather than taking the turn into the grocery store parking lot. Then just keep following the main road for quite a ways and you will eventually see the Rodney Bay Mall on your left.

Take a left and follow the road out until it nearly ends. You will see a sign for Spinnakers by the Police Station. Turn left into a big parking lot and park. Walk over to the beach and look at it so that you can tell everyone you've seen it. It's miles long and is pretty but sometimes is crowded with lots of tourists. Spinnaker's is a funky beach bar that's fun and you may just end up there for lunch.

Otherwise, go back to the main road and go left. Pass the Rodney Bay Marina on your left. Continue straight ahead. Eventually, the road narrows and you will find a big sweeping turn to the right. There's a little sign there that says Cap Maison and you will take a left rather than the sweeping right-hander. The resort is down a little bit on the right. Cap Maison is a terrific view restaurant and you can often see Martinique across the channel.

After lunch stop in the Marina for some boat watching and some ice cream at Elena's and then, it's back to Marigot Bay for "Toes Up". Later this afternoon, you may wish to do the sunset cruise as a fitting way to top off your St. Lucian adventure. There are several options in the Bay but our favorite is run by the Chateau Mygo folks. You will have your own Captain and Mate and snacks and drinks are included. It leaves around 4 PM and you'll be back right after sunset, which is a little after 6 PM in the winter months.

## Day 7 (Time to head back home to reality)

You may want to have lunch at the Fox Grove Inn (758-455-3800) on the way to the Hewanorra airport...another one of our favorite places. It's on the side of a mountain overlooking the ocean and is about 45 minutes away from Marigot Bay.

As you leave Marigot Bay, take a left and then, a quarter of a mile past the grocery store, take a right. You'll be retracing the steps you took when you arrived. About 30-45 minutes into your trip, you'll be in a sort of flat area and you'll see a sign by a banana plantation to the Fox Grove Inn. Don't take this. Keep going straight up the hill to the second Fox Grove Inn sign and turn right.

Esther will take good care of you and please give her our regards. They are famous for their salads. Personally, I like the Mamiku Salad that has sausage, tomatoes, lettuce and cheese with a mustard sauce. Yummy and unique. Gale likes the Farmhouse Salad that is more conventional with bacon and things. If neither appeals, they have a great fishplate called the Trio of fish in a Pernod sauce...delicious.

The airport check in is relatively straightforward. Just drop off the car and proceed to your airline's counter. The security is pretty tight and you may be "selected" to have your bag opened and inspected on a random basis. We know that they advise that you be there 3 hours ahead of time but we've found that two hours is adequate.

Once through security, there is a large waiting area that, sometimes, can be hot. There are the usual duty free shops, etc. in the waiting area. You'll also find a flight of steps up to the second level. There's food up there and it's a good idea to grab something for the long flight home.

As you're waiting for your flight to be called, wander over to a little stand or kiosk with a sign that says "Quality Foods". Buy a jar of the Mango Jam...it's delicious and when you get back home, it will remind you of the terrific time you spend in this beautiful, friendly country.

# CONCLUSION

When we first visited St. Lucia, we were amazed at the country's natural beauty...it's mountains and clear waters. But more importantly, we were impressed with its people. St. Lucians are just plain happy people. They may not have a lot of things but they know their island is special and they take pride in it. They are friendly and courteous. Their culture emphasizes love and hospitality. They dress well and their children wear uniforms to school. You will seldom hear a child crying or demanding that their parents buy them candy.

We wrote this book to help point you in the right direction so that you will have a pleasurable experience on the island. We hope you enjoyed the book and that it was useful. If so, we would appreciate a favorable review at your favorite retailer's website.

Thank you and we hope you have a pleasant stay on beautiful St. Lucia...

Gale and Gerry Bay

August 2018

# ABOUT THE AUTHORS

Gale and Gerry Bay live in Jamestown, RI and have four children and ten grandchildren between them.

Gale and Gerry have sailed since they were children. They have raced and cruised a Frers 41 and later, cruised a Hylas 54. During 2003-5 they sailed the Caribbean aboard their Hylas and they fell in love with St. Lucia. Deciding to put down roots there, they purchased an apartment as part of the Marigot Bay Resort and Marina. They use their apartment 6 weeks out of the year and then, at other times, it is part of the rental pool at the resort. During their visits to the island, they have become intimately familiar with its sights and its culture.

Recently, they made the move to a powerboat. They own a Back Cove 29 called Ragtime. While they are sailors at heart, they enjoy the ease and convenience of a powerboat.

When not on the boat, Gerry can be found flying radio-controlled airplanes or using his ham radio. Gale is involved with charitable work and, of course, the grandkids!

They maintain a family website,

http://www.channelbells.com and can be reached at:

27 Newport St.
Jamestown, RI 02835

# OTHER BOOKS BY GALE AND GERRY BAY

Gale and Gerry wrote and published, "Sailing the Caribbean Islands" about their sailing adventures. They sailed their Hylas 54, Windsong, from Rhode Island to the Caribbean for two years and this book chronicles their adventures and the interesting characters they met along the way. It is available in multi-media format as an iBook and in paperback and Kindle formats from Amazon.

Gerry also wrote the book, The SS North American". One of the last cruise ships on the Great Lakes, Gerry was the Radio Operator aboard the ship during the summer of 1960. The book chronicles his adventures as the ship rescued a pleasure craft, survived grounding on a sandbar in the St. Lawrence River and survived a nasty storm on Lake Michigan. He describes the ship's and the era's history and relates tales about life onboard including his sighting of a flying saucer.

Also available from the iBooks Store is Gerald Ballou Bay's Genealogy. Gerry is related to several Kings and other interesting characters including Chief Canonicus of the Narragansett Indian tribe and the famous pirate, Thomas Tew. This book contains photos, biographies and lineage of some of the characters in Gerry's background.

# PHOTO GALLERY

## Rodney Bay

Figure 1: Beautiful Reduit Beach at Rodney Bay is about 2 miles long

Figure 2: You can buy Roti's, an island delicacy, right on the beach.

Figure 3: Spinnakers, right on Reduit Beach, is a fun place to eat.

Figure 4: Spinnakers looks across Rodney Bay towards Pigeon Island

# Rodney Bay (Continued)

Figure 5: Fruit is delivered right to your boat or to the Beach by a fun local guy

Figure 6: View of Pigeon Island from Cap Maison

Figure 7: Sunset at Rodney Bay

Figure 8: Michelle Elliott's beautiful pottery can be found in the shops at Rodney Bay and elsewhere on the island.

# Castries

Figure 9: Buying vegetables in the Castries Market

Figure 10: School children on a field trip to the Castries Market

Figure 11: Bringing home a fish for dinner

Figure 12: View of Castries Harbor from the Pink Plantation House.

# Marigot Bay

Figure 13: View of Marigot Bay looking to the Southeast.

Figure 14: Rainbow over Marigot Bay viewed from one of the Marigot Bay Resort's apartments

Figure 15: View of Marigot Bay from an apartment deck at the Marigot Bay Resort and Marina.

Figure 16: Mega Yachts tied up at the Marina offer insights into the lifestyles of the rich and famous.

## Marigot Bay (Continued)

Figure 17: The Marigot Bay Beach

Figure 18: Boats for rent on the Marigot Bay Beach.

Figure 19: Anse La Raye, near Marigot Bay, is a colorful fishing village.

Figure 20: Sava leaves the Pitons on the way back to Marigot Bay

# Pitons

Figure 21: The Pitons jut right up from the water.

Figure 22: A rainbow marks the Sugar Beach Resort at the base of the Pitons.

Figure 23: A turnoff on the road to Soufriere is a great place to get a view of the Pitons.

Figure 24: Sugar Beach at the base of the Pitons is beautiful.

# Pitons (Continued)

Figure 25: Colorful houses in the fishing village of Canaries shine in the late afternoon sun.

Figure 26: Steam arises from the Caribbean's only drive-in volcano.

Figure 27: The Island's rugged interior can be enjoyed on the road from Marigot Bay to the Pitons.

Figure 28: View of the Pitons from the deck of the Dasheen Restaurant at the Ladera Resort

# Snorkeling

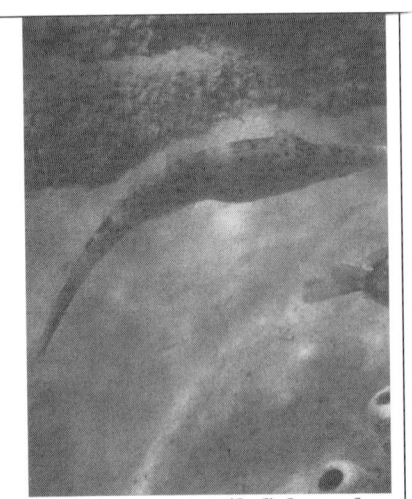

Figure 29: A Filefish and a Doctor Fish glide by some tube coral.

Figure 30: Anse Chastanet has spectacular Elkhorn Coral.

Figure 31: An Octopus blends in with the coral.

Figure 32: Squid tend to swim in formation.

Printed in Great Britain
by Amazon